LIBYA

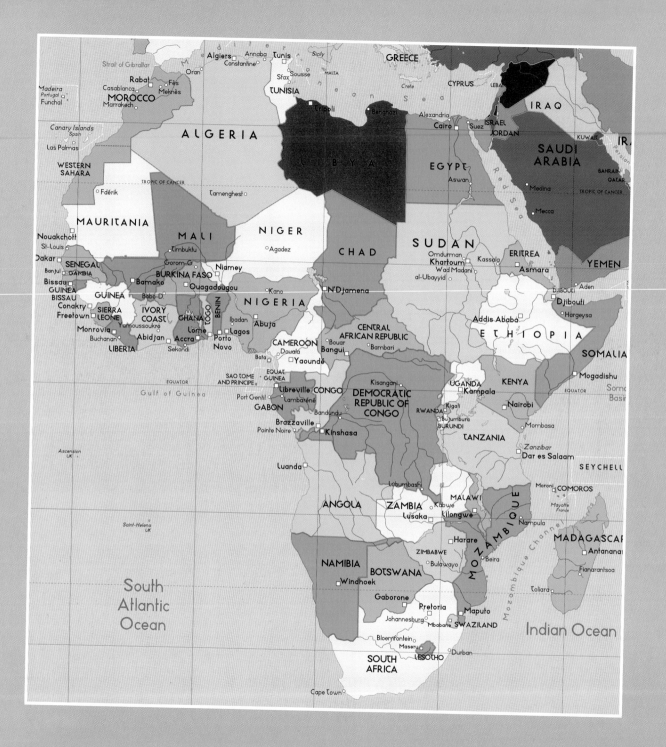

LIBYA

Judy Hasday

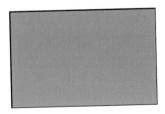

Mason Crest Publishers
Philadelphia

Produced by OTTN Publishing, Stockton, N.J.

Mason Crest Publishers
370 Reed Road
Broomall, PA 19008
www.masoncrest.com

First printing

1 3 5 7 9 8 6 4 2

Library of Congress Cataloging-in-Publication Data

Hasday, Judy L., 1957-
 Libya / Judy Hasday.
     p. cm. — (Africa : continent in the balance)
 Includes bibliographical references and index.
 ISBN-13: 978-1-4222-0083-4 ((hc))
 ISBN-10: 1-4222-0083-3 ((hc))
 1. Libya—Juvenile literature. I. Title.
DT215.H345 2007
961.2—dc22

                              2007011705

Africa: Facts and Figures
The African Union
Algeria
Angola
Botswana
Burundi
Cameroon
Democratic Republic
 of the Congo

Egypt
Ethiopia
Ghana
Ivory Coast
Kenya
Liberia
Libya
Morocco
Mozambique

Nigeria
Rwanda
Senegal
Sierra Leone
South Africa
Sudan
Tanzania
Uganda
Zimbabwe

Table of Contents

Africa: Continent in the Balance
Robert I. Rotberg

Africa is the cradle of humankind, but for millennia it was off the familiar, beaten path of global commerce and discovery. Its many peoples therefore developed largely apart from the diffusion of modern knowledge and the spread of technological innovation until the 17th through 19th centuries. With the coming to Africa of the book, the wheel, the hoe, and the modern rifle and cannon, foreigners also brought the vastly destructive transatlantic slave trade, oppression, discrimination, and onerous colonial rule. Emerging from that crucible of European rule, Africans created nationalistic movements and then claimed their numerous national independences in the 1960s. The result is the world's largest continental assembly of new countries.

There are 53 members of the African Union, a regional political grouping, and 48 of those nations lie south of the Sahara. Fifteen of them, including mighty Ethiopia, are landlocked, making international trade and economic growth that much more arduous and expensive. Access to navigable rivers is limited, natural harbors are few, soils are poor and thin, several countries largely consist of miles and miles of sand, and tropical diseases have sapped the strength and productivity of innumerable millions. Being landlocked, having few resources (although countries along Africa's west coast have tapped into deep offshore petroleum and gas reservoirs), and being beset by malaria, tuberculosis, schistosomiasis, AIDS, and many other maladies has kept much of Africa poor for centuries.

Thirty-five of the world's 50 poorest countries are African. Hunger is common. So is rapid deforestation and desertification. Unemployment rates are often over 50 percent, for jobs are few—even in agriculture. Where Africa once was a land of small villages and a few large cities, with almost everyone

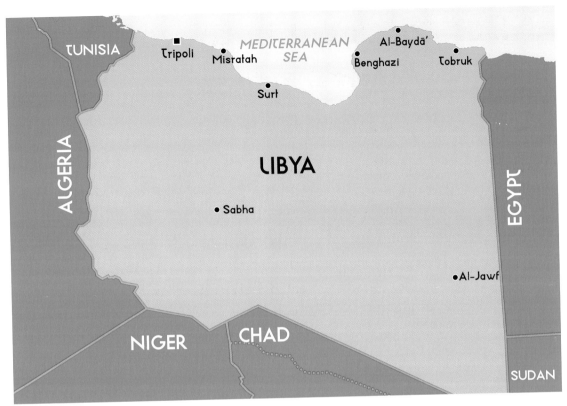

The North African country of Libya contains vast reserves of oil beneath its arid desert sands.

engaged in growing grain or root crops or grazing cattle, camels, sheep, and goats, today more than half of all the more than 900 million Africans, especially those who live south of the Sahara, reside in towns and cities. Traditional agriculture hardly pays, and a number of countries in Africa—particularly the smaller and more fragile ones—can no longer feed themselves.

There is not one Africa, for the continent is full of contradictions and variety. Of the 750 million people living south of the Sahara, at least 130 million live in Nigeria, 74 million in Ethiopia, 62 million in the Democratic Republic of the Congo, and 44 million in South Africa. By contrast, tiny Djibouti and Equatorial

A mural painting of Mu'ammar Gadhafi looms over passersby in Tripoli. Gadhafi has ruled the country of Libya since 1969.

Guinea have fewer than 1 million people each, and prosperous Botswana and Namibia each are under 2.5 million in population. Within some countries, even medium-sized ones like Zambia (11.5 million), there are a plethora of distinct ethnic groups speaking separate languages. Zambia, typical with its multitude of competing entities, has 70 such peoples, roughly broken down into four language and cultural zones. Three of those languages jostle with English for primacy.

Given the kaleidoscopic quality of African culture and deep-grained poverty, it is no wonder that Africa has developed economically and politically less rapidly than other regions. Since independence from colonial rule, weak governance has also plagued Africa and contributed significantly to the widespread poverty of its peoples. Only Botswana and offshore Mauritius have been governed democratically without interruption since independence. Both are among Africa's wealthiest countries, too, thanks to the steady application of good governance.

Aside from those two nations, and South Africa, Africa has been a continent of coups since 1960, with massive and oil-rich Nigeria suffering incessant periods of harsh, corrupt, autocratic military rule. Nearly every other country on or around the continent, small and large, has been plagued by similar bouts of instability and dictatorial rule. In the 1970s and 1980s Idi Amin ruled Uganda capriciously and Jean-Bedel Bokassa proclaimed himself emperor of the Central African Republic. Macias Nguema of Equatorial Guinea was another in that same mold. More recently Daniel arap Moi held Kenya in thrall and Robert Mugabe has imposed himself on once-prosperous Zimbabwe. In both of those cases, as in the case of the late Gnassingbe Eyadema in Togo and Mobutu Sese Seko in Congo, these presidents stole wildly and drove entire peoples and their nations into penury. Corruption is common in Africa, and so are weak rule-of-law frameworks, misplaced development, high expenditures on soldiers and low expenditures on health and education, and a widespread (but not universal) refusal on the part of leaders to work well for their followers and citizens.

Conflict between groups within countries has also been common in Africa. More than 15 million Africans have been killed in the civil wars of Africa since 1990, with more than 3 million losing their lives in Congo and more than 2 million in the Sudan. Since 2003, according to the United Nations, more than 200,000 people have been killed in an ethnic-cleansing rampage in Sudan's Darfur region. In 2007, major civil wars and other serious conflicts persisted in Burundi, the Central African Republic, Chad, the Democratic Republic of the Congo, Ivory Coast, Sudan (in addition to the mayhem in Darfur), Uganda, and Zimbabwe.

Despite such dangers, despotism, and decay, Africa is improving. Botswana and Mauritius, now joined by South Africa, Senegal, and Ghana, are beacons of democratic growth and enlightened rule. Uganda and Senegal are taking the lead in combating and reducing the spread of AIDS, and others are following. There are serious signs of the kinds of progressive economic policy changes that might lead to prosperity for more of Africa's peoples. The trajectory in Africa is positive.

Libya is an arid country with no permanent rivers or waterways. (Opposite) Sand and gravel seas of the Sahara Desert cover about 90 percent of the country. (Right) A shepherd allows his sheep to graze amid sparse vegetation, near the construction site of the Great Man-Made River, a major irrigation project.

1 Treasure in the Sand

AHLAN WA-SAHLAN! That's the word for "welcome" in Arabic, the major language of Libya. It is an ancient land, with a past that is among the oldest in recorded history. Until it achieved independence in 1951, Libya was made up of separate, diverse tribes and groups that over the centuries were absorbed into various empires and kingdoms. United more than 50 years ago into an independent nation, Libya is still undergoing development today. Much of that growth is being driven by oil—huge reserves lie just beneath the surface of the land. They have allowed the people of Libya the opportunity to transform their country from one of the poorest in the world to one of the wealthiest.

Libya is strategically located in the center of Africa's northern coast, with Algeria and Tunisia to the west; Egypt to the east; and Sudan, Chad, and Niger to the south. Just across the Mediterranean Sea to the north lie the

Quick Facts: The Geography of Libya

Location: Northern Africa, bordering the Mediterranean Sea, between Egypt and Tunisia
Area: slightly larger than Alaska
  total: 679,358 square miles (1,759,540 sq km)
  land: 679,358 square miles (1,759,540 sq km)
  water: 1,618 square miles (4,190 sq km)
  Borders: Algeria, 610 miles (982 km); Chad, 656 miles (1,055 km); Egypt, 693 miles (1,115 km); Niger, 210 miles (354 km); Sudan, 238 miles (383 km); Tunisia, 285 miles (459 km); coastline, 1,091 miles (1,770 km)

Climate: Mediterranean along coast; dry, extreme desert interior
Terrain: mostly barren, flat to undulating plains, plateaus, depressions
Elevation extremes:
  lowest point: Sabkhat Ghuzayyil, -154 feet (-47 m)
  highest point: Bikku Bitti, 7,438 feet (2,267 m)
Natural hazards: hot, dry, dust-laden *ghibli* is a southern wind lasting one to four days in spring and fall; dust storms, sandstorms

Source: CIA World Factbook, 2007.

major countries of Europe. Libya's 679,358 square miles (1,759,540 square kilometers) make it the fourth-largest country on the African continent and the 17th-largest in the world. This vast territory is larger than the state of Alaska.

The Desert and the Sea

About 90 percent of Libya's land is part of the Sahara Desert, the world's largest desert. It covers about 3.5 million square miles (9 million sq km), or about one third of the African continent. The Sahara is bordered on the west by the Atlantic Ocean, to the north by the Atlas Mountains and the Mediterranean Sea, to the east by the Red Sea, and to the south by the *Sahel* region.

Many picturesque images of the Sahara highlight its swirling, rippled sand dunes, which can be immense in size. One mass of sand dunes known as Libyan Erg is as large as the country of France. About 70 percent of the Sahara, however, is composed of rocky plains covered with stones and gravel. A few limestone *plateaus* complete the desert topography.

The sandy and rocky wilderness of the Sahara Desert makes up much of Libya's interior. It contains miles of flat gravelly areas disrupted by occasional plateaus that rise up from the sand. The desert is an extremely dry

This NASA satellite image of August 2001 shows a massive dust storm over Libya. Hot dry winds carrying particles of dust and sand blow off the Sahara to the north for days at a time.

environment that does not support much life. However, there are isolated fertile areas with reliable water resources that are scattered throughout the land. The presence of water in these *oases* makes it possible for travelers to safely pass across the otherwise desolate region.

In sharp contrast to the barren landscape of Libya's interior is the country's northern coastline. Extending 1,000 miles (1,600 km) along the Mediterranean Sea, it boasts beautiful beaches and fertile land. The coastal lowlands and highland *steppes* of this part of the country contain the *arable* soils vital to Libya for agricultural production.

Cyrenaica, Tripolitania, and Fezzan

Libya has historically been divided into three distinct regions, each separated from the other by geographical barriers such as plateaus or desert. The largest of these regions, covering about half of the country, is called Cyrenaica. It includes the northeastern coast of Libya and extends southward into the desert. The desert of southwestern Libya is known as the Fezzan region, while the northwestern coastal area is called Tripolitania. Both Cyrenaica and Tripolitania are separated from one another by the Gulf of Sidra and by a region of barren desert called Sirtica. Plateaus separate the two regions of Cyrenaica and Tripolitania from Fezzan.

Cyrenaica contains the Akhdar Mountains, a forested, fertile area that extends for about 100 miles (161 km) along the northeastern coast of Libya. These limestone mountains, located inland from the coast, rise to heights of about 2,000 feet (609 meters), with the highest elevation reaching 3,000 feet (914 m). The mountain range includes a narrow coastal plateau called Jabal

Al Akhdar, which contains the cities of Al-Marj and Darnah. In central Libya, the Al-Haruj al-Aswad Plateau rises up about 2,600 feet (792 m). It is composed of fine grain basalt rock and capped by volcanic peaks.

The desert region known as Fezzan has some agricultural oases, such as the Marzuq Basin. In the far southwestern part of Libya, bordering Algeria, the Acacus Mountains rise up from the desert. Although it covers more than one fourth of the country, the Fezzan contains only a small percentage of Libya's population.

Libya's smallest geographical region—Tripolitania—contains the most people. Located along the extreme northwestern Mediterranean coast of Libya, Tripolitania also supports much of the country's agriculture. Most farming takes place in a fertile coastal lowland area called the Al-Jifarah Plain, which encompasses about 10,000 square miles (25,900 sq km). It also is the site of Libya's capital and largest city—Tripoli. Further south, the Nafusah Plateau rises up from the plain, reaching heights ranging from 1,500 to 3,200 feet.

A Variable Climate

Libya's climate varies depending upon the location. Along the Mediterranean coast the weather is usually warm and humid, especially during the months of July and August. In the summer, temperatures around Tripoli average from 72°F to 85°F (22°C to 29°C). Further east along the coast in the Cyrenaica region, the city of Benghazi has average temperatures that range from 62°F to 86°F (17°C to 30°C). During the winter months of January and February, the climate is cooler. Winter temperatures in Tripoli average

تونس
طرابلس
سرت
خليج سرت
بنغازي
بو قرين
درنة
بن جواد
اجدابيا
السويرح
طبرق
جالو
حقل السرير
مصر
حقل تازربو
الكفرة

المرحلة الأولى
المرحلة الثانية
المرحلة الثالثة

A map of the Great Man-Made River. Considered one of the largest engineering feats in the world, this irrigation project is carrying water from aquifers beneath the Sahara Desert to Libya's populous coastal regions.

around 47°F to 61°F (8°C to 16°C), while temperatures in Benghazi are slightly warmer, at 50°F to 63°F (10°C to 17°C).

The Sahara Desert region has much more extreme conditions. In the summer, temperatures rise as high as 122°F (50°C) during the day, while winter temperatures barely reach above freezing (0°C). It is not uncommon to see frost and snowfalls in the mountain areas.

The harsh, dry, climate in the Sahara is rendered even worse by the *ghibli*, a hot, dusty wind that blows up from the south many times over the course of the year. The *ghibli* carries sands and dust that have been churned up from the desert. When this wind blows, particles in the air make the sky appear red, and can cut visibility down to about only 60 feet (18 m).

Water is scarce in Libya. The dry sands of the Sahara receive less than 3 inches (7.6 cm) of rain each year. However Libya's Mediterranean coast does get some precipitation. In the

Tripolitania and Cyrenaica regions 8 to 15 inches (20 to 38 cm) of rain falls each year.

Libya has no permanent rivers or streams, but its dry riverbeds and waterways, called *wadis*, fill with water after heavy rains. To trap this water in reservoirs, the government has constructed networks of dams in the *wadis*. People also obtain water from wells. In order to tap into another potential water source—the subterranean *aquifers* that exist beneath the Sahara Desert—the Libyan government has developed the Great Man-Made River. Begun in the 1980s, the massive irrigation project consists of a series of pipelines that carry water from the Sahara to the Libyan coast.

Animal and Plant Life

Despite the lack of water and the wide variations of temperature typical of the desert, some animal life survives. One of the most widely known animals of the desert is the camel. Because it can store about 50 gallons (189 liters) of water in three different parts of its stomach, this mammal can go for up to 10 days without water. On its back is a large hump of stored fat that it can access when no other food is available. The pack animal of choice used for centuries by traders, merchants, and other travelers crossing the desert, the sturdy camel can carry more than 1,000 pounds (454 kg) of weight.

Another animal commonly found in the Sahara is the jerboa, a mouse-like creature that comes out to feed during the cooler temperatures of night. Jerboas are also a source of food for predators of the desert, which include fennec foxes, hyenas, and wildcats. Desert oases provide environments for other small animals, such as mice, rats, and even some types of bats.

For many centuries the Arabian camel provided an efficient means of transportation for people traveling through the hostile environment of the Sahara Desert.

Although they were once abundant in Libya, gazelles and antelopes are now found only in small numbers due to overhunting. The *wadden*, a male gazelle that is the national animal of Libya, can be found in the northern coastal regions. Along the western border with Algeria, small numbers of the *addax* antelope still survive.

After the heat of the day has passed, a variety of desert reptiles and arthropods typically come out at night to search for food. The Sahara is home to many different species of spiders, centipedes, grasshoppers, beetles, snakes, and lizards. One of the largest scorpion species in the world, the emperor scorpion, also lives in desert burrows in Libya.

Only a few species of birds, such as vultures, hawks, and grouses, can survive in the harsh desert environment. Smaller birds, including warblers, larks, and turtledoves, can be found around the oases, where there is some water and vegetation.

Except for the scrubby grasses scattered amid the sand, plant life is minimal in the desert. Most vegetation is found in the oases, which typically contain palm trees and cacti. People who live in the desert weave the leaves, or fronds, of the palm tree into useful products such as baskets and sandals. They eat the palm tree fruit, or dates, fresh off the tree or dry it for later use. Desert people living in oases also obtain food from the prickly pear cactus, which grows a sweet, juicy fruit.

When there is sufficient rainfall, the coastal regions and highlands support various kinds of grasses, scrub vegetation, and trees such as the juniper or lentisk (mastic tree). Among the many hardy grasses that grow on the plains is esparto grass, which is used for making paper and rope. At one time, it was a major export of Libya.

(Opposite) Moammar Gadhafi has headed the government of Libya during most of its history as an independent country. (Right) The remains of a theater in the ancient Roman city of Leptis Magna, near Tripoli. From the first century B.C. until the late fourth century A.D. the Roman Empire controlled much of the Mediterranean region, including Libya.

2 From Colony to Nation

LIBYA IS A NATION of two histories. The first is the story of its tribes, regions, and cities that over the centuries were conquered and occupied by various empires, ranging from the Greeks and Romans to the Arabs and Italians. The other is the history of a country that gained its independence and established itself as a new, sovereign nation.

An Ancient Past

Libya has been inhabited for many centuries. *Archaeologists* have discovered rock paintings and engravings carved by a prehistoric people that date back to around 10,000 years ago. These ancient works of art, which have been found in all three regions of Libya—Tripolitania, Cyrenaica, and Fezzan—do not portray a desert land. Instead, the rock paintings and carvings depict

These images dating from 10,000 years ago were found in caves of the Acacus Mountains of southwestern Libya, near the border with Algeria.

lush, green vegetation and a variety of animals roaming near flowing rivers and lakes in a region that is now desert.

Artifacts that date from about two thousand years later give some idea about a culture that developed along the Libyan coastal plain between 7400 B.C. and 6000 B.C. The people of this society were farmers, who grew crops and raised cattle that grazed in the grassland plains. This early culture thrived for several thousand years until the area began to dry up and become desert.

Around the time that the land was changing from fertile land to arid desert, a group of people began to migrate into North Africa from the Middle East. By 2000 B.C. these people—known as the Berbers—had established settlements along the Mediterranean coast and in Saharan oases. The Berbers eventually covered a vast region that reached from Egypt, in northeastern Africa, to the Niger Basin, in the west-central part of the continent.

The Phoenicians

Libya's location along the Mediterranean's shores made it a desirable area for *maritime* cultures. From harbor cities along the region's coast, ships could easily travel and trade with European countries to the north, as well as with North African countries to the east and west.

Around 1000 B.C. the Phoenicians (a seafaring culture based in today's Lebanon) began arriving on Libya's shores, where they established ports along the coast. They did not set up permanent communities in the region, nor did they explore much in the interior.

However, the Phoenicians did found a port city to the west, in present-day Tunisia. Called Carthage, the city expanded its control into neighboring territories, eventually developing into a wealthy empire. By the fifth century B.C. Carthage had become the Phoenicians' greatest colony. At that time the Carthaginian Empire controlled much of the North African coast along the Mediterranean Sea, including the region of Libya known as Tripolitania.

Greeks and Romans

Like other Mediterranean maritime cultures, the Greeks also established ports along the North African coast. In 631 B.C. they founded the city of Cyrene in northeastern Libya, in what is now known as the Cyrenaica region. Other settlements within this area came later, including Barce (Al Marj) and Euhesperides (Benghazi).

Greek colonies established along the western coast of Libya eventually fell to Carthage. And around the first century B.C. the eastern settlements fell to the Egyptians, who had established a kingdom in the fertile Nile River Delta.

During the third and second centuries B.C., a series of wars broke out between the Carthaginian Empire and Roman Empire as each fought for the other's territory. These conflicts, which came to be known as the Punic Wars, ended in 146 B.C., when the Romans destroyed the city of Carthage. Subsequently, the Roman Empire established a stronghold in the Tripolitania region.

With the defeat of the Egyptians in Cyrenaica in 96 B.C., the Roman Empire established control over much of the territory that makes up today's Libya. As the Romans expanded their influence in the region, they built grand cities and monuments that reflected the economic and political power of their empire.

Islam Comes to Libya

Although the Roman Empire dominated the region for the next several hundred years, the Empire weakened during the late fourth century A.D. and split apart into western and eastern halves. The Western Roman Empire eventually fell to barbarian tribes, which included the Vandals, a Germanic warrior people. The Vandals swept through other Mediterranean lands, and during the 400s occupied Libya. However, in 535 they were driven out by the armies of the Eastern Roman Empire, also known as the Byzantine Empire. Like the Vandals, the Byzantines maintained control for only about a hundred years. The next group that took over Libya—the Arabs—would have a more permanent presence.

In 639 Arab armies invaded North Africa, bringing with them a new religion. The Arabs came as conquerors and as disciples to spread the word and religion of Islam, a religion founded in the early 600s A.D. by the Prophet Muhammad (ca. 570–632). His followers became known as *Muslims*, which means "those who submit" to the will of God, or Allah.

Muslim Arabs invaded Libya around 642 and began to convert many of the region's *indigenous* Berber people to Islam. The Arabs required the conquered people to speak their language and abide by their Islamic law, called *Sharia*. Some Berber people resisted the Arab authority, and fled into the desert, where they preserved their own language and culture. By the 11th century, however, most of the people of Libya had become Muslims.

While Arab control of Libya lasted only about 500 years, the occupation had a lasting impact on the people and culture. No other invading people

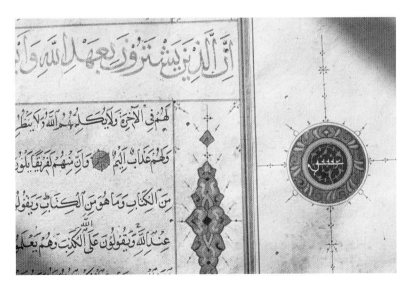

A manuscript page from the Islamic holy book the Qur'an. When Muslim Arabs invaded the Mediterranean region of Libya in the 600s, they converted most of the indigenous people to the religion of Islam.

were as significant in shaping 21st century Libya. Both the religion and the language introduced by the Arabs more that one thousand years ago are predominantly practiced and spoken in the country today.

Islam and the Ottomans

During the 12th century, the Arabs lost control of the region. Over the next several centuries, Libyan land changed hands frequently as Islamic forces

Barbary Coast governments forced countries such as the United States to pay tribute to keep their merchant ships from being attacked by pirates. In the early 1800s, when the U.S. government refused to pay, the ruler of Tripolitania declared war. This engraving shows U.S. Navy ships bombarding the coastal fortifications in Tripoli. The city was captured by American marines in 1805.

from various countries, including Morocco, Tunisia, Egypt, and Spain, occupied the region.

During the 15th and 16th centuries the Ottoman Empire, based in Turkey, spread throughout the Middle East and North Africa. Turkish control over the North African Coast, also known as the Barbary Coast, allowed the Ottoman Empire to grow wealthy through trade and piracy. Nations were forced to pay tribute to prevent pirate attacks on merchant ships, and they had to pay ransom when ships were captured. Such practices continued until the latter part of the 19th century.

Around the beginning of the 20th century, Italian leaders decided that possession of the Ottoman provinces of Tripolitania and Cyrenaica would give Italy control of significant seaports along the Mediterranean Sea. In 1912, aware that the weakened Ottoman Empire did not have the ability to hold on to its North African territories, Italian forces easily drove the Turks from the region.

Under Italian Rule

While under Ottoman rule, the people living in Cyrenaica had formed a resistance organization called the Muslim Nationalist Force. It was led by Omar Mukhtar, a Muslim of the Senussi religious brotherhood. After Tripolitania and Cyrenaica became colonies of Italy, Mukhtar's group turned to fighting against the Italian occupation.

In 1914, when the First World War broke out, Italy fought alongside Great Britain and France against Germany and Turkey. Mukhtar and his *mujahedeen* (Arabic for "strugglers," but which has also come to mean "freedom fighters") joined with the Turks to fight the Italians.

After the war, which ended in 1918, Italy instituted a bloody and ruthless forcible response to the Muslim resistance. From 1929 to 1931 more than 100,000 Libyans were rounded up by Italian authorities and detained in concentration camps. An estimated 750,000 Libyans fled the country or died during this time. The resistance continued until 1931, when Mukhtar was wounded and captured during a skirmish with Italian forces. The aged tribal leader was tried and hanged. His death brought an end to any further resistance.

In the years that followed, Italy established some economic initiatives to develop the Libyan colonies. The government instituted programs to improve roads, develop water irrigation systems, and increase crop production. However, many of these improvements were made not to help Libya's indigenous people, but to encourage Italians to immigrate to the colonies.

Italy's efforts to colonize the region were interrupted by World War II (1939–1945). At that time, Italy sided with Germany and Japan. Known as the Axis powers, these countries fought against the Allied forces, which included Great Britain, Free France, and the United States. During the six-year conflict, which raged over Europe, the Pacific, and North Africa, hundreds of thousands of soldiers and civilians from dozens of countries around the world were killed or wounded. Libya was the site of significant battles between the Axis and Allied forces.

The people of Libya recognized that their best chance for independence from Italy rested on the success of the Allied forces. In 1943, the Libyan Arab Force (made up of Sanussi volunteers) helped British and Free French armies take control of the Cyrenaica region from the Germans and Italians. Two years later, after the war ended, the United Nations determined that Libya would no longer be a colony. After being temporarily placed under UN administration, the country would be granted independence in 1951, and ruled as a constitutional *monarchy*.

King Idris

Libya's leader, Mohammed Idris Al-Senussi, was chosen by a national assembly to rule over the country, which was called the United Kingdom of Libya. Idris appointed a governor to head the three regional provinces of Tripolitania, Cyrenaica, and Fezzan. The cities of Tripoli (in Tripolitania) and Benghazi (in Cyrenaica) were both designated as capitals.

King Idris maintained close ties with the industrialized countries of Western Europe and the United States (often referred to collectively as "the West"). He allowed the United States and Great Britain to establish military

King Idris I (1890–1983) ruled Libya from 1951 to 1969. The head of the Senussi Muslim religious order, Idris had waged guerilla warfare against Italian colonial rule in the 1930s and 1940s. During World War II, he led the Libyan Arab Force, which fought with U.S., British, and Free French armies in North Africa.

bases in Libya. When oil was discovered in the country in 1959, Western foreign companies provided expertise and training to help develop the industry.

However, Libya faced many problems. Almost 90 percent of all Libyans were *illiterate*, and there were few tradespeople or technically skilled citizens, doctors, or teachers. Under King Idris, some improvements in healthcare and educational systems were made, but these programs typically benefited only a select group of the wealthy and politically influential. Even after the oil industry began to bring huge amounts of money into the country, most of the wealth went to a politicized urban elite made up of the royal family and its supporters. Poverty was widespread.

In September 1969, the Free Officers Movement ousted King Idris from power in a bloodless coup d'etat. The movement was led by a 12-member Revolutionary Command Council headed by Colonel Mu'ammar Gadhafi, shown here in this 1969 photograph.

Discontent with Idris's rule led a 27-year-old captain named Mu'ammar al-Gadhafi (also spelled al-Qaddafi) to lead a *coup d'état* on September 1, 1969. Along with a group of military men, who called themselves the Free Unionist Officers, Gadhafi seized power while Idris was out of the country.

A Break with the West

Promoted to colonel and declared commander-in-chief of the Libyan military,

Gadhafi assumed leadership of the country. He introduced a form of Arab *socialism*, in which the state owned key sectors of the economy. Accordingly, he nationalized foreign-owned property and businesses, including the oil industry. Distrustful of the West, he closed the British and U.S. military bases in Libya that had been established under Idris.

Gadhafi was an *Arab nationalist*. In the early 1970s, in an attempt to create a united Arab world, he signed on to several treaties with other Arab nations. When these efforts failed, Gadhafi turned to supporting various factions and *insurgent* groups fighting against Arab governments that opposed him. He used brutal methods and violence against his opponents, even sending out death squads to pursue those living in exile. During the 1970s and 1980s, using oil revenues, Gadhafi built up Libya's military forces with tanks, aircraft, and helicopters, supplied by France at first and later by the Soviet Union.

Mu'ammar al-Gadhafi's actions made him unpopular with Arab countries and in the West. Tensions between his government and the United States spiked in 1981 when two Libyan aircraft were shot down after challenging American warplanes flying over the Gulf of Sidra. A year later, the United States imposed trade restrictions against Libya.

Countries in the West, including the United States and Great Britain, linked several terrorist incidents to the Libyan government, including the bombing in 1986 of a discotheque in Berlin, Germany, often visited by U.S. soldiers based nearby. In response to the Berlin attack, the U.S. government carried out a series of bombing raids on Libyan military facilities and residential areas in Tripoli and Benghazi.

Two years later, Libyan terrorists were accused of planting a bomb aboard Pan Am Flight 103, which blew up over Lockerbie, Scotland, killing 270 people. Gadhafi refused to surrender the Libyan suspects to the United States and Great Britain, so in 1992 the United Nations imposed *sanctions* against the North African nation. The United States and many other countries continued to consider Libya a dangerous state that was inciting terrorism around the world. They were also concerned that Libya was developing a nuclear weapons program.

Wreckage from Pan Am Flight 103 litters the ground of Lockerbie, Scotland. The 747 had been on its way to the United States in December 1988 when a bomb planted by Libyan terrorists exploded, killing all 259 passengers aboard and 11 Scottish citizens on the ground.

Reestablishing Ties

After sanctions isolated Libya from the rest of the world, the government began to reevaluate its relationship with the West. During the late 1990s and early 2000s Libya's government appeared to change its policies.

In response to accusations of terrorism, the Libyan government agreed to cooperate with investigations in the Pam Am bombing. In April 1999 the two Libyan suspects were turned over to the West. In January 2001, a special court in the Netherlands found one of the suspects, Abdel Basset Ali al-Megrahi, guilty of the bombing. The other suspect, Lamen Khalifa Fhimah, was found not guilty and set free.

In August 2003, in a letter addressed to the United Nations Security Council, Libya accepted full responsibility for the Pam Am Flight 103 bombing. The Libyan government agreed to pay $2.7 billion to the families of its victims. Soon afterward, the United Nations Security Council voted to lift UN sanctions. The following year Libya agreed to pay $35 million to the families of victims of the 1986 Berlin disco bombing.

The United States refused to lift its own economic sanctions against the country, citing Libya's nuclear weapons program as a reason not to resume normal relations. However, in December 2003 Gadhafi announced that Libya would end its development of biological and chemical weapons, discontinue its nuclear arms program, and allow international weapons inspectors into the country.

(Opposite) Judge Abdallah Aoun (far right), president of the Libyan Correctional Court, reads a statement at a hearing in June 2005. (Right) A shop displays various language editions of Moammar Gadhafi's Green Book. The volume contains an explanation of the Libyan leader's political philosophy, which he calls the Third Universal Theory.

3 Green Book Governance

LIBYA'S OFFICIAL NAME is the Great Socialist People's Libyan Arab Jamahiriya. The word *jamahiriya* in Arabic means a "state representing the interests of the great masses." Libya's current government was established in March 1977, when its constitution was passed.

Socialism and Islam

After Colonel Muammar al-Gadhafi led the coup d'état in 1969 that ousted King Idris from power, a new government was established, called the Libyan Arab Republic. Headed by a 12-member Revolutionary Command Council, the government lasted less than a decade. Gadhafi wanted to create a new structure of government—one that combined socialism and Islam.

Gadhafi rejected *capitalism* and *communism*, finding both political systems failures. Capitalism refers to the economic and political system found in the United States. Under capitalism, individuals own property and run businesses for profit. The government does not control the production or distribution of goods—instead, market forces drive the economy. Communism, on the other hand, is a form of socialism, in which the government or the people own the country's businesses and industries. Under socialism, the government controls the production and distribution of goods, in theory for the benefit of the people. Under communism, a political system associated with the People's Republic of China and the former Soviet Union, power lies with the Communist Party.

Third Universal Theory

A devout Muslim, Gadhafi rejected the West's presence in the Arab world. He envisioned a Libya economically and politically free of the West, a reuniting of Libya with the rest of the Arab world, and a government based solely on Islamic law. Under Gadhafi, the Libyan constitution is based on laws of the Qur'an, the holy book of Islam. It is the religious law that sets the tone for all other laws. For example, drinking alcoholic beverages and gambling are forbidden in the Qur'an, so there is no legal gambling or alcohol consumption permitted in Libya.

Gadhafi calls his political system the Third Universal Theory. He describes it in a publication simply called the Green Book. Green is the symbolic color of Islam, and Gadhafi's Green Book outlines his vision of an Islamic-based socialist government in which all the people hold power. He considers the government structure he has established in Libya to be a form of "direct democracy."

People's Committees and Congresses

All Libyans age 18 or older must participate in the election of councils called people's committees. These exist at local through national levels. For elections at the local level Libya is divided into 25 municipalities, called *baladiyat* (singular, *baladiyah*). These municipalities are further divided into 186 zones, in which every citizen is a member of a Basic Popular Congress. Each Basic Popular Congress has a secretariat, or elected leadership committee. Called the People's Committee, this body administers the local government of the zone.

At the national level is the General People's Congress, which meets several times a year. More than 1,000 delegates serve within the Congress, whose members come from lower-level committees, congresses, and professional unions. It is similar to a parliament in that it is responsible for passing laws and determining other forms of legislation.

The General People's Congress is headed by a five-member General Secretariat, which was initially headed by Gadhafi in the role of secretary general. In 1979 he resigned the position, but has continued for almost 40 years in an untitled position as ruler of Libya. There is also a national-level General People's Committee, with each member in charge of a department of the government.

The legal system in Libya is based on the Italian civil law system and Islamic law. Local courts address issues concerning personal, criminal, civil, and commerical law. Political issues are handled by people's courts, revolutionary courts, and military courts. The high court is the Supreme Court, followed by lesser judiciary bodies such as the Courts of Appeal, the Courts of First Instance, Summary Courts, and the People's Court.

Controversial Leader

Despite Gadhafi's claim to have created a society in which there is a "direct democracy," he has assumed ultimate power in Libya. Because he has the support of the military, he can easily fend off any attempts to overthrow him. Some people believe Gadhafi to be no more than a dictator, who by having banned all political parties has essentially pre-

A Libyan People's Committee meeting. Because he believes that the people's will is expressed through such "popular congresses" Gadhafi considers political parties unnecessary and has banned them.

vented any opponents from having a voice in government.

Others see Gadhafi as a strong leader who has improved life for all Libyans. They note that under his rule, money revenues from oil exports have been invested back into the country in the form of new schools, better healthcare, and improvements to the country's *infrastructure*.

Gadhafi's Third Universal Theory called for a "new economic order" based on a more equitable division of wealth between developed and underdeveloped countries. Accordingly, the theory justified his country's aggressive foreign policy, which included sponsorship of numerous terrorist and guerrilla movements throughout world.

In the late 1990s Gadhafi changed his approach with Western nations and has taken action to improve his country's relations with the international community. As a result, the United Nations and the United States have lifted several damaging sanctions against Libya that were causing economic hardships for much of the general population.

International Outreach

Despite the fact that many questions have been raised about Libya's record in human rights, in January 2003 the country was elected to chair the UN Commission on Human Rights. The outcome has been protested by many human rights groups, which report that people are detained without cause in Libya and often mistreated while imprisoned.

In addition to being a member of the United Nations, Libya belongs to several other international organizations. It is a member of the League of Arab States (Arab League), Organization of Arab Unity (OAU), Organization of Petroleum Exporting Countries (OPEC), and Organization of Arab Petroleum Exporting Countries (OAPEC).

In 2005 Libya held its first auction of oil and gas exploration licenses. This event marked the return of American energy companies in Libya for the first time in more than 20 years. In May 2006 the United States and Libya officially restored full diplomatic ties.

(Opposite) A pipe fabrication plant located in Sarir, Libya, as seen through one of its products: a massive underground water conduit used in building the Great Man-Made River. (Right) The $5.6 billion Mellitah treatment plant, which processes natural gas produced from Libyan oil fields and pumps it to Sicily, Italy, via a 323-mile (520-km) subsea pipeline.

4 Black Gold Economy

LIBYA'S ECONOMY IS UNIQUE among the countries of North Africa. Unlike the nearby countries of Algeria, Tunisia, Morocco, and Egypt, Libya does not have the water resources and amount of arable land needed to support an agricultural economy. As a result, the country must import about 75 percent of its food. The nation's greatest resource is the "black gold" found under the desert sand—oil.

Libya's Oil

Before 1959, a lack of natural resources left Libya struggling economically. However, after the first oil well gushed its black crude to the surface, Libya went from being one of the poorest nations in the world to one of the wealthiest. Crude oil—the unprocessed oil that is pumped out of the ground—is a

Quick Facts: The Economy of Libya

Gross domestic product (GDP*): $74.97 billion

Inflation: 3.1%

Natural resources: petroleum, natural gas, gypsum

Agriculture (7.3% of GDP): wheat, barley, olives, dates, citrus, vegetables, peanuts, soybeans; cattle

Industry (51.3% of GDP): petroleum, iron and steel, food processing, textiles, handicrafts, cement

Services (41.4% of GDP): retail, government, financial

Foreign trade:
Exports–$37.02 billion: crude oil, refined petroleum products, natural gas, chemicals

Imports–$14.47 billion: machinery, semi-finished goods, food, transport equipment, consumer products

Economic growth rate: 8.1%

Currency exchange rate: U.S. $1 = 1.28 Libyan dinars (2007)

*GDP is the total value of goods and services produced in a country annually.
All figures are 2006 estimates unless otherwise indicated.
Source: CIA World Factbook, 2007.

fossil fuel—developed naturally from decaying plants and animals that lived millions of years ago. Once crude oil is refined, or processed, it can be used in a variety of ways. It serves as fuel for cooking and heating, and as gasoline fuel for automobiles.

Huge profits can be gained from selling crude oil to nations like the United States, which consumes about 20 million barrels of oil a day. A barrel of crude oil holds about 42 gallons (159 liters). When refined into gasoline, one barrel of crude produces about 19 or 20 gallons (75 liters) of gasoline. Supply and demand on the world market determines how expensive a barrel of oil is—the prices change from day to day. In early 2007, the average price of crude oil was $56 per barrel.

Since the discovery of oil at Jebel Zelten, several other oil fields across Libya have been found. One area with significant oil reserves is the Surt Basin, a region in the Sahara a few hundred miles southeast of the Gulf of Sidra. The largest oil field in Libya is Sarir, which is located in the southern Cyrenaica region of the country. Other important oil fields include Amal, Gialo, Nasser (Zelten), Defa, Augila, Hateiba, Messla, Raguba, and Bahi.

Libya's oil industry has produced huge revenues. The country's 80 oil fields collectively generate 1.4 million barrels of oil each day. Just eight of these fields alone produce about a million barrels a day. That amounts to between $6 and $8 billion annually.

Limited Agriculture

Only about 1.2 percent of Libya's land can be used for farming. Most of it takes place along the Mediterranean coast of the Tripolitania and Cyrenaica regions, although some occurs in the Fezzan area, near oases. Libyan farmers grow cereals, such as wheat and barley, as well as other crops, such as olives, watermelons, almonds, citrus fruits (oranges, dates, apricots, and figs), tomatoes, potatoes, onions, and tobacco. Almost all crops are grown for use within Libya, and not for export.

Since Libya has very little water for agricultural use, tapping into underground freshwater reserves, or aquifers, has become an important undertaking. In 1984, in an effort to provide much-needed irrigation to

Libya's land, making more of it suitable for growing crops, construction of the Great Man-Made River (GMR) began. One of the largest engineering projects undertaken in the world, the massive project involved connecting 13-foot-wide and 23-foot-long concrete pipes and placing them below the desert sand. Today, more than 3,100 miles (about 5,000 km) of pipeline carry 230 million cubic feet (6.5 million cubic meters) of water per day from more than 1,000 desert wells. Most of these aquifers are found in four underground basins in the Sahara—the Kufra, Surt, Morzuk, and Hamada Basins. In 1993, GMR pipes brought water to the city of Benghazi, and three years later, to Tripoli. Today, water from the system is available in most of Libya's coastal cities.

The Libyan government estimates that when completed the Great Man-Made River will bring water to approximately 320,0000 acres (130,000 hectares) of farmland. Construction of the massive project to date has cost $20 billion.

Livestock and Fish

Raising livestock is another important part of Libya's agricultural production. Before the discovery of oil, the sale of livestock and its products played a vital part in Libya's economy.

Camels, horses, mules, and donkeys are still used for transporting some goods across the desert and from one region of the country to another. Some animals are raised for their hides and hair, which are used to make clothing, blankets, and tents. Goats, cows, and camels provide milk that is also used in making cheese products. Under Libya's system of government, dairy farms

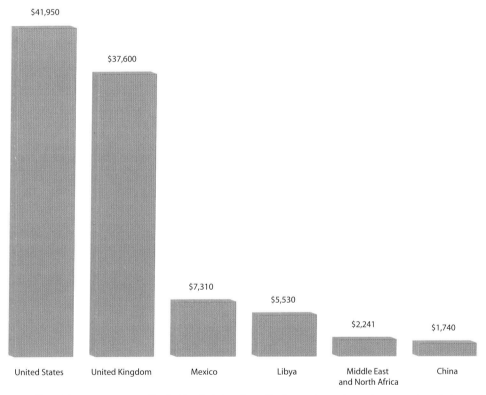

Gross National Income (GNI) Per Capita of Libya and Other Countries*

- United States — $41,950
- United Kingdom — $37,600
- Mexico — $7,310
- Libya — $5,530
- Middle East and North Africa — $2,241
- China — $1,740

*Gross national income per capita is the total value of all goods and services produced domestically in a year, supplemented by income received from abroad, divided by midyear population. The above figures take into account fluctuations in currency exchange rates and differences in inflation rates across global economies.

Note: These figures were calculated by the World Bank using the Atlas methodology, which reduces the impact of exchange-rate fluctuations when comparing the incomes of several countries.

Figures are based on 2005 data. Source: World Bank, 2006.

are privately owned and operated, but owners are required to sell the milk to the state. Some livestock, such as sheep, goats, cattle, and chickens, are raised as a source of meat.

Despite the fact that Libya has more than 1,000 miles (1,600 km) of coastline along the Mediterranean Sea, fishing is not a major industry. The waters off Libya's coast do not contain much fish because the waters are low in plankton (the tiny organisms that serve as food for other small sea creatures). Some commercial fisherman, however, do work off the shores near Tripolitania, where they net mostly sardines, red mullet, and tuna. Sponge beds are also harvested, although mostly by Greeks who are permitted to do so by licenses issued by the Libyan government.

Manufacturing and Industry

Libya's oil industry drives the nation's economy. Employment in this sector is higher than in any other sector of the economy. Many Libyans earn good wages working in oil-industry-related jobs.

The downside to focusing so much on oil production is that there is very little manufacturing present in Libya. There are some small factories in the country, primarily in the large urban cities such as Tripoli and Benghazi. However, most of these factories, which typically produce processed foods, beverages, cement, leather goods, and textiles, tend to be small operations that employ fewer than 100 people. Some factories manufacture products such as tanks, pipe fittings, and steel drums that serve the needs of the oil industry.

Geologists predict that Libya's oil reserves will be depleted within the 10 to 12 years. Because oil wells will eventually stop spouting the "black

Libyan women solder parts of computer and television circuit boards at an electronics plant in Zawiyah. The country's manufacturing industries unrelated to oil are typically small. The majority of them involve the processing of agricultural products, production of building materials, and creation of textiles and handicrafts.

gold" for the economy, Libyans will need to further develop other industries to keep the nation's economy flourishing. The challenges ahead will be to determine what those industries will be and how to best make them viable alternatives.

(Opposite) In the narrow streets of Tripoli's old city, or medina, vendors display their wares. (Right) Berber women from Kabaw, in northwestern Libya, pose in their traditional clothing and jewelry.

5 A Blend of Peoples

EVEN THOUGH LIBYA is located on the continent of Africa, the nation is considered part of the Arab world. This term is used to describe the 323 million people who live in 22 different countries but share a common language—Arabic.

Historically, the people of Libya identified themselves by the region in which they lived: Cyrenaica was dominated early on by the Bedouin tribes who brought the Arab culture with them during the 11th century. The Berbers living in Tripolitania were Arabized later so that area contained more Berbers, while the desert region of Fezzan remained sparsely populated, with pockets of minority ethnic groups. Only after independence did the people of these three regions begin to refer to themselves as Libyans.

Quick Facts: The People of Libya

Population: 5,900,754 (note: includes 166,510 non-nationals)

Ethnic groups: Arab and Berber, 97%; Greeks, Maltese, Italians, Egyptians, Pakistanis, Turks, Indians, Tunisians

Age structure:
0–14 years: 33.6%
15–64 years: 62.2%
65 years and over: 4.2%

Birth rate: 26.49 births/1,000 population

Infant mortality rate: 23.71 deaths/1,000 live births

Death rate: 3.48 deaths/1,000 people

Population growth rate: 2.3%

Life expectancy at birth:
total population: 76.69 years
male: 74.46 years
female: 79.02 years

Total fertility rate: 3.28 children born/woman

Religions: Sunni Muslim 97%

Languages: Arabic (official), Italian, English

Literacy: 82.6% (2003 est.)

All figures are 2006 estimates unless otherwise indicated.

Source: Adapted from CIA World Factbook, 2007.

Ethnic Groups

Most of Libya's 5.9 million citizens consider themselves to be Arabs. However, the majority of them—97 percent of the population—actually have a mix of Arab and Berber ancestry. The people of Libya all speak Arabic, but many also speak local *dialects* (variations of a common language). Classical Arabic, which is the official language of all Arab nations, is taught in the schools.

Although Libyans of combined Arab and Berber ancestry make up most of the country's total population, there are several other ethnic groups living in the country. Among them are Africans from the interior of the continent, whose ancestors were brought centuries earlier to the Fezzan and Tripolitania regions to work as slaves. Many ethnic Europeans and Asians also live in Libya, including Greeks, Maltese, Italians, Pakistanis, Turks, and Indians. Ethnic Africans living in Libya also come from the adjacent countries of Egypt and Tunisia. Most foreigners work in Libya's petroleum business and in the construction of the Great Man-Made River. Today, a blend of peoples from more than 100 nations lives in Libya.

Nomads

Although the majority of Libya's people live in the coastal region of the country, several ethnic groups live in the desert. Most of these tribes live in oasis settlements. However, some desert dwellers are *nomads*—people who move from place to place, with their camels, and herds of goats and sheep, in search of grazing areas and water holes. Some nomadic tribes have lived in the deserts of Libya for many centuries.

Nomads rely on their livestock for everything from food to transportation. Because they move from place to place so often, they rarely accumulate things beyond what meets their immediate needs. Nomads live in tents that are set up near or around desert oases, where they can obtain water and trade with settlers or the other nomads they meet.

Some Libyans lead a *semi-nomadic* lifestyle, in which they live permanently in an area where they cultivate crops. However, their housing consists of portable or temporary shelters, and they move their livestock from place to place in order to provide grazing lands and water.

The Berbers

While the Berbers living in the coastal regions of Libya have assimilated into the Arab culture, tribes living in the desert regions have maintained their traditions and language. The majority of them live in oasis settlements, although there are some nomadic tribes.

One distinct Berber tribe is the Tuareg, of southwestern Libya. In the past, the Tuaregs were primarily warriors and traders who engaged in the trans-Saharan trade, using camel caravans. As methods of transportation across the desert have changed—trade is now mostly done by plane or cargo vehicles—many of the Tuareg camel caravans have disappeared.

The Tuareg are sometimes referred to as the "Blue People" because the indigo blue dye used in their traditional clothing stained the wearer's skin dark blue. Today, the Tuaregs typically dress in a variety of colors, but still turn to their traditional, blue-dyed clothing for special occasions and celebrations.

At their gatherings, the Tuareg, whose heritage is rich in poetry and music, pass on their legacy through song. Musical instruments are often brought and played at many Tuareg functions. Elderly women often play the moncord violin, or *Anzad* at an evening ceremony known as *Takket*.

The majority of Tuaregs practice the Islamic faith, although women do not cover their faces with a veil, a practice typical of many Muslim women. Instead it is the Tuareg men who traditionally cover their faces—except for their eyes—and also wrap a cloth around their heads into a turban. Although the veil provides some protection against the harsh Sahara winds and sand, it is worn more out of a sense of tradition. Many Tuareg also carry amulets that contain verses of the Islamic holy book, the Qur'an.

Today some Tuareg people are settled farmers, while others live as nomads, herding camels, sheep and goats. Although once vast in numbers, the Tuareg population has dwindled due to a severe drought in the 1970s and 1980s.

Bedouins

Another nomadic people, but of Arab ancestry, are the Bedouins. The word *Bedouin* comes from the Arabic word *badawi*, which means "one who lives in the desert." Bedouins are the descendants of Arab invaders and the native Berber population of North Africa. Found mostly in the Cyrenaica region, they speak various dialects of the Arabic language.

A Tuareg man rides his camel in the Sahara Desert. The Tuaregs are a traditionally nomadic desert people who live in southwestern Libya, around the oasis towns of Ghat and Ghadames.

For many centuries the Bedouins lived in the desert as nomads, moving from place to place in search of grazing areas and water. Today, most are not traditional nomads; some work in cities or towns. Others lead a semi-nomadic life, growing barley and wheat crops on the Jabal Al Akhdar plateau. Just south of the plateau, the desert is dotted with several oases, including Jalu and Jaghbub, where herders take their sheep, goats, and cattle to graze.

The Bedouins who still live as traditional nomads have a harsh life. They may travel from 12 to 40 miles a day in the desert, where temperatures reach as high as 125°F (51.6°C) during the day and fall as low as 40°F (4°C) at night. The Bedouins live in tents and depend on their animals to provide dairy products for food and hides for clothing and shelter. They typically travel in large extended-family units, and are fiercely loyal to their tribes.

Religion

Nearly all of Libya's almost 6 million people (97 percent of the population) follow the Islamic faith. Their holy book is the Qur'an, which is Arabic for "recitation," or "written material that is repeated from memory." The majority of Libyans are Sunni Muslims, which is the dominant branch of Islam around the world. Only a small minority of Libyans are Shiites, the other major branch of Islam.

The Islamic religion is based on five principles, called the five pillars of Islam. They are: *shahada*, a statement of faith; *salat*, daily prayer; *zakat*, giving charity to those in need; *sawm*, fasting during the Islamic month of Ramadan; and *hajj*, pilgrimage to the holy city of Mecca. Prayer is an essential part of living a Muslim life. Muslims pray five times a day facing in the direction of Mecca, the holiest city of Islam, located in Saudi Arabia.

Although Islam is the religion practiced by most of Libya's people, the country does have citizens who practice other faiths. There are about 50,000 Christians living in Libya, most of whom are Roman Catholics. At one time more than 30,000 Jews lived in Libya, but they fled when Gadhafi gained power. There is still a small Jewish presence; some returned after the Great Synagogue and a Jewish school were rebuilt in Tripoli. There are also a few Hindus, Baha'is and Buddhists in the country, but no known places of worship for them. Other religions include the Anglican, Coptic, and Greek Orthodox faiths.

Education

Today's Libya has a high literacy rate, especially when compared to most other countries in Africa. More than 75 percent of Libyans age 15 and older can read and write. This high level of literacy has come about because the government subsidizes education—it is free at all grade levels for Libyans.

By law, all children ages 6 through 15 must attend school. Young children in elementary grades attend classes together, but once they are older, boys and girls are separated. After students enter intermediate school, they typically focus on learning the Qur'an, the Arabic language, Islam, and the subjects of history, geography, and science. Libya also has several technical schools that offer vocational training in such fields as agriculture and technology.

Libya has several universities and colleges that offer higher educational opportunities. Garyounis University in Benghazi features programs in science,

At a school in Tripoli, Muslim boys review the Arabic alphabet. Gadhafi's government has placed great emphasis on education, which is compulsory and free for all Libyans. As a result, the country has one of the highest literacy rates of African nations—92 percent for males and 72 percent for females, according to 2003 estimates.

engineering, dentistry, and agriculture, while the University of Al-Fatah in Tripoli offers training in subjects ranging from petroleum and minerals, to economics, to law, and to medicine.

Arts and Recreation

The Libyan government encourages many of the country's traditional arts and crafts, including dance, weaving, wood-carving, metalworking, and embroidery. Libyan craftspeople create a variety of handicrafts that are sold in cities like Tripoli and Benghazi in open-air marketplaces called *souks*. There, metalsmiths create and sell copper, gold, and silver jewelry. Artisans also craft and sell items such as baskets, carpets, rugs, leatherwork, and pottery in these city marketplaces.

Sports events are very popular in Libya. Many people enjoy watching horse or chariot races. There are also camel races, which in southern Libya involves a competition between the riders, measuring their skills as well as the speed of their *mehari* camels. Along the northern regions of Libya, in its larger cities, sports enthusiasts enjoy playing golf or tennis. Further north, along the coast, popular pastimes include swimming, diving, and water skiing.

Perhaps the most popular sport in Libya is soccer, also called football. Boys and young men play on organized teams or with friends on city streets, village grounds, and desert oases. Many schools host organized teams and competitions. Libya has also a national team that has participated in the African Cup of Nations, a tournament held every two years to determine the soccer championship of Africa. Libya hosted the event in 1982, when its team came in second. The country is scheduled to host the event again in 2014.

(Opposite) A view of downtown Tripoli. Libya's largest city contains about one third of the country's population.
(Right) For many centuries, the oasis town of Ghadames in sparsely populated southwestern Libya served as an important caravan center on the trans-Saharan route from Tripoli to West Africa.

6 Swirling Sand to Coastal Sea

ALMOST 90 PERCENT of Libya's almost 6 million people live in about 10 percent of the country's land—in the cities and towns in the nation's Mediterranean coastal lowlands. Even in ancient times, when Libya was part of other empires, most of the population settled in the regions bordering the sea. Today the most prominent cities in this area include Tripoli, Benghazi, Misratah, and Tobruk. In the desert region of Fezzan, the city of Sabha is the most important city beyond the coastal region.

Tripoli

Tarabalus Al-Gharb, or "Tripoli of the West" as it is sometimes known, is the capital of Libya, as well as the nation's largest city and chief seaport. The seat of the Gadhafi's national government, the city houses official bureaus, as well as office buildings, theaters, hotels, and restaurants. Modern Tripoli has experienced huge growth since the 1970s, when extensive restoration programs were undertaken.

Located on the northwestern coast of the country, Tripoli is the commercial center of Libya. Much of Tripoli's economy revolves around the agricultural production in the area. Among the major crops that are brought to market in Tripoli are olives, fresh vegetables, citrus fruits, tobacco, and grains. The busy seaport and international airport handle a great deal of traffic, especially since the lifting of sanctions by the United Nations and the United States. More than 1.8 million people live in the city, which blends parts of the ancient and the modern world.

Tripoli was founded by the Phoenicians in the seventh century B.C. Over time, control of the port city changed hands many times. Remnants of its ancient past can be seen in the old city, known as the medina. Constructed during the Roman-controlled period, the medina was enclosed by walls built to protect the city from invaders. Within the old city is the white marble Arch of Marcus Aurelius, which the Romans built during the second century A.D. to honor their emperor. Today, it is the only remaining Roman monument left in Tripoli.

The medina also contains *souks*, where merchants sell their wares, and seven *mosques*, including the Gurgi and Karamaly Mosques. Both are noted for their intricate tile work and ornate decoration. Another outstanding structure from Tripoli's history is the 16th-century Spanish Castle Assaraya Al-Hamra, or Red Castle. Once the home of the ruling families, it still dominates the city skyline. Tripoli is also home to University of Al-Fatah.

There are a number of archeological sites just outside Tripoli. The most well-known and visited site is Leptis Magna (sometimes spelled Lepcis Magna). Located east of Tripoli, Leptis Magna was the largest of three great Roman cities of the ancient region of Tripolitania. The other two were Tripoli (Oea) and Sabratha (Sabratah). Some of the ruins in Leptis Magna date to the second century A.D. They include the Severan Arch, the Hadrianic Baths, the Colonnaded Street, the Severan Forum, the Temple of Rome and Augustus, and the Arch of Tiberius.

Benghazi

Benghazi once served with Tripoli as the co-capital of Libya. Located in the Cyrenaica region, the port city sits on the northeast coast of the Gulf of Sidra. With a population of more than 725,000, it is about half the size of Tripoli and ranks as the second-largest city in Libya.

Founded by the Greeks in the sixth century B.C., Benghazi was ruled by five different empires before the Italians gained control in 1911, after the Turko-Italian War. During

The Tripolitania region was named for the "three cities," or *tripolis* (from Greek), that dominated in ancient times: Oea (today's Tripoli), Sabratha, and Leptis Magna. Today, Leptis Magna, located outside Tripoli, is famous as an archeological site. It contains some of the world's best-preserved Roman ruins, including the statue and theater shown here.

Located in the northeastern Cyrenaica area of Libya, on the Gulf of Sidra, Benghazi is the country's second-largest city.

World War II, Benghazi was bombed more than 1,000 times by European forces. As a result, little of its ancient heritage remains.

Today, Benghazi's economy centers around industries such as salt- and food-processing, oil refining, cement manufacturing, tanning, and sponge and tuna fishing. The city is also a vital oil port: petroleum from nearby oil fields is pumped directly to the city for export. Other export products include sponges, animal hides, and wool. Benghazi is the site of Garyounis University, which was founded in 1955.

Misratah

The third-largest city in Libya, with a population of more than 184,000 people, Misratah is located in the northwestern part of the country, east of Tripoli. Separated from the Mediterranean Sea by a stretch of sand dunes to the north, Misratah is a coastal oasis with an abundant water supply underground. Originally known as Thubaqt, the town of Misratah developed around the seventh century as a caravan supply center. By the 20th century, it had become an important agricultural region. Large groves of date palms and olive trees can be found throughout the city.

The Arab architectural influence can be seen in the older section of Misratah, which has narrow arched or covered streets. In the modern part of the city, public garden and tree-lined avenues enhance Turkish and European-style buildings.

During the 20th century, the Italians developed the harbor area and financed the establishment of a large iron and steel mill—both facilities have helped strengthen the city's economy. Misratah is also well-known for its colorful carpets and textiles, as well as for its factory-produced baskets and pottery. The city is an educational center, with several seminaries, a technical college, and an institute for teacher training.

Tobruk

At the far reaches of the northeastern coast of Libya is Tobruk. Its deep, protected natural harbor makes the city one of the best seaports along the Mediterranean Sea and vital to Libya as a trade and transportation center. Tobruk is especially valuable to Libya's oil industry: a pipeline carries crude oil from one of the major wells inland to the port, where it is then exported to countries around the world. Tobruk also has a major oil refinery, where processing of crude oil takes place.

Because of Tobruk's strategic location along the coast, the city changed hands many times as the Allies and the Axis Powers fought over the city during World War II. The harbor and an airfield 15 miles (24 km) south of the seaport made Tobruk an ideal location from which to launch military offensives and for use as a base of operations. Some of the most prolonged fighting in North Africa took place in Tobruk. Several World War II cemeteries containing the remains of both Allied and German soldiers can be found in this Libyan city.

Sabha (Sebha)

Located in an oasis of central Libya, the city of Sabha is the capital of the Fezzan region. Noted for its wide streets and pristine white buildings, Sabha is a lush and colorful city, where vegetation thrives in the middle of the

Sahara Desert. Because of its central location, Sabha serves as an important transportation hub. Travelers heading through Libya from the neighboring African countries of Niger, Chad, and Algeria typically stop over in Sebha to replenish food and water supplies.

The oasis region surrounding Sabha is fertile and supports crops such as barley, wheat, onions, and dates. Because the date harvest is typically strong, a factory for processing and packing this fruit was built in the city.

Sabha's 40,000 people work mainly in administrative, trade, transportation, and tourism businesses. Because the outlying desert area is used as a site for missile and rocket launch testing, the Libyan military has a strong presence.

A Calendar of Libyan Festivals

March

On March 2, Libyans observe **Declaration of the People's Authority Day**, also known as **People's Power Declaration**. It commemorates the day the Great Socialist People's Libyan Arab Jamahiriya was founded in 1977.

UK Evacuation Day is observed on March 28. On that date in 1970 British troops evacuated from all military bases in Libya.

June

U.S. Evacuation Day is observed on June 11. It commemorates the date in 1970 that U.S. troops withdrew from foreign military bases in Libya.

August

Armed Forces Day falls on August 11. The day honors the Libyan Arab Force, which was founded in exile in 1940.

September

The anniversary of the Sept 1, 1969, coup d'état that ousted King Idris I and brought Gadhafi into power is celebrated each year on **National Day**, also called **Revolution Day**. The holiday is celebrated with parades, military displays, and public speeches.

October

October 7, formerly known as **Constitution Day**, marks the date in 1951 that the Libyan constitution for the Kingdom of Libya was adopted. The holiday was renamed **Fascist Evacuation Day** in 1970, and the day now commemorates the eviction of the last Italian settlers in Libya. The suffering that Libyans endured under Italian colonial rule is remembered each year on October 26, which is Libya's Day of Mourning, or Mourning Day.

December

Libya recognizes the date that the United Nations voted to grant the country independence in 1951 with the political holiday of **Independence Day**, celebrated on December 24.

Religious Observances

As a Muslim country, Libya observes several holy days related to the Islamic religion. Major celebrations occur according to the lunar calendar, in which the months correspond to the phases of the moon. A lunar month is shorter than a typical month of the Western calendar. Therefore, these festivals fall on different dates each year.

A very important month of the Muslim lunar calendar is the ninth month, **Ramadan**. This is a time of sacrifice for devout Muslims. During Ramadan, Muslims are not supposed to eat or drink between sunup and sundown. They are also supposed to restrict their activities during these hours to necessary duties, such as going to work. After the sun has set completely, Muslims make a special prayer before eating a small meal. Muslims mark the end of Ramadan with a celebration called **Eid al-Fitr**, or "breaking of the fast." During this time families get together and exchange gifts.

A Calendar of Libyan Festivals

Eid al-Adha (the Feast of the Sacrifice) takes place in the last month of the Muslim calendar during the **hajj** period, when Muslims make a pilgrimage to Mecca. The holiday honors the prophet Abraham, who was willing to sacrifice his own son to Allah (God). In the story, God provided a sheep to be sacrificed instead. According to tradition, Muslim families slaughter and eat a sheep on this day. On Eid al-Adha, families traditionally eat a portion of the feast and donate the rest to the poor. The day before Eid al-Adha—the **Day of Arafa**—is also recognized as a holiday in Libya.

Another holy day is **Mouloud**, or the birth of the Prophet. Muslims celebrate this day with prayer and often a procession to the local mosque. Families gather for feasts, which often feature the foods said to have been favored by Muhammad: dates, grapes, almonds, and honey. The holiday falls on the 12th day of the third month of the Islamic calendar, known as **Rabi'-ul-Awwal**.

Muslims also celebrate **El am Hejir**, the Islamic New Year. It falls on the first day of the first month (called Muharram) of the Islamic calendar.

In Libya, the Muslim holy days of the Day of Arafa, Eid al-Adha, El am Hejir, Eid al-Fitr, and Mouloud are national holidays.

Recipes

Recipes

Sharba Libiya (Libyan Soup)

1/3 to 1/2 lb. lamb meat, cut into small pieces
1/4 cup oil
1 large onion
1 Tbsp. chopped fresh parsley
1 Tbsp. tomato paste
2 or 3 tomatoes, chopped
1 lemon
1/2 cup orzo (rice-shaped pasta)
Salt, red pepper, Libyan spices (*hararat*) or cinnamon
Crushed dried mint leaves
Lemon juice

Directions:
1. Sauté the onion and meat in oil.
2. Add parsley and sauté until meat is brown.
3. Add chopped tomatoes, tomato paste, salt and spices, and stir.
4. Add enough water to cover meat, and then simmer on medium heat until meat is cooked.
5. Add more water if needed, and bring to a boil.
6. Add orzo; simmer until cooked.
7. Before serving, sprinkle crushed dried mint leaves, and squeeze fresh lemon juice to taste.

Variations:
Substitute chicken or beef for lamb.
Add uncooked soaked chickpeas with the meat.
Add cilantro with parsley.

Aseeda

4 cups rye flour
6 1/2 cups water
1/2 cup yeast
1 tsp. salt
honey

Directions:
1. Mix flour, 2 cups of water, and yeast in a bowl.
2. Leave mixture in a warm place for five hours.
3. Bring 4 cups of water and the salt to a boil.
4. Add the aseeda mixture and mix with a wooden spoon.
5. After the mixture thickens (add more flour if dough does not thicken), add 1/2 cup water and simmer.
6. Pour into a bowl, and let stand until cool and thick.
7. Turn upside down onto a plate and cover with honey.

Ghreyba (Butter Cookies)

1 cup warm *samn* (clear butter fat)
1/2 cup powdered sugar
3–4 cups of flour
almonds

Directions:
1. Mix *samn* and sugar well.
2. Add flour gradually and mix.
3. Shape into small balls and press down gently to flatten into shape.
4. Garnish with an almond.
5. Bake in a preheated oven at 400°F (200°C) for 10 to 15 minutes.

Mhalbiya (Rice Pudding)

5 cups of whole milk
5 heaping Tbsp. rice flour
1 cup sugar
3 to 5 Tbsp. orange blossom water
Cinnamon or crushed nuts

Directions:
1. In a saucepan add the sugar to 4 cups of milk and let it warm up gently on low-medium heat to speed up the dissolution process.
2. Add rice flour to the remaining cup of milk and stir it well, until there are no lumps.
3. Gradually pour flour-milk mixture into the saucepan, stirring constantly and very gently on low heat, until the mixture starts to bubble.
4. Mix in the orange blossom water.
5. Pour mixture into small custard dishes and cool to room temperature.
6. Garnish with a sprinkle of ground cinnamon or crushed nuts.

Adapted from http://www.libyana.org/food/

Glossary

aquifer—freshwater waterway that lies beneath the land.

Arab nationalist—one who believes in the unification of all Arab-speaking people under one government.

arable—suitable for growing crops.

archaeologist—a scientist who studies past human life as seen in fossils and the structures and tools left by ancient peoples.

capitalism—a political and economic system in which individuals own property and run businesses for profit and the government does not control the production or distribution of goods.

communism—a political and economic system in which the government owns all property and businesses and equally distributes goods to the people.

coup d'état—a sudden or violent overthrow of a government, often with the aid of the military.

dialect—a regional variety of a language, in which the grammar, vocabulary, and pronunciation differ from that of the same language as spoken in other areas.

fossil fuel—energy source that comes from prehistoric plant and animals.

ghibli—a hot, dust-laden wind of northern Africa that blows from the south out of the Sahara Desert.

illiterate—unable to read or write.

indigenous—originating in a specific region or location.

infrastructure—services and facilities such as roads, electricity, telephone service, and public transportation that support the economic activity of a country.

insurgent—one who fights against an established government.

maritime—of or relating to the sea.

monarchy—rule or governance by a king (monarch).

mosque—a Muslim house of worship.

nomads—wandering people, often herders who move from place to place to find pastures and water for their livestock.

oasis—(plural, *oases*) an isolated fertile area near a reliable source of water in the desert.

plateau—a level plain located above sea level.

sanction—an economic or military measure placed on a nation by a group of countries in an effort to bring about policy change.

Sahel—a dry region that lies between the Sahara Desert to the north and more fertile savanna regions to the south.

semi-nomad—a person based in a permanent location, but who migrates from place to place with livestock in search of grazing lands and water.

Sharia—Islamic law.

socialism—a political and economic system in which the government owns business and industry and supervises the distribution of goods.

souk—a marketplace in northern Africa; also refers to a stall found in a marketplace.

steppe—dry, level, and grass covered land.

wadi—dry riverbed filled occasionally and temporarily by rainwater.

Project and Report Ideas

Comparative Map

Research information on major deserts of the world. Make five photocopies of a map of the United States. Then make a photocopy of the maps of five different subtropical deserts chosen from the list below (be sure to use maps from the same source so they are the same scale).

Sahara Desert (Africa)	Arabian Desert (Middle East)
Kalahari Desert (Africa)	Gibson Desert (Australia)
Mohave Desert (USA)	Sonoran Desert (USA)
Chihuahuan Desert (Mexico)	Thar Desert (India, Pakistan)

Cut out and paste the five U.S. maps on a 16- x 20-inch poster board. Then cut out the maps of the five desert areas and paste each on top of one of the U.S. maps. Label your display with the name of each desert and its size in square miles. Write a short caption that compares and contrasts the sizes of each desert in relation to the size of the United States.

Essay Report

The Arabian camel has been an important animal for people living in the desert. Research facts about the Arabian camel—its size, weight, coloring, and any special features or characteristics that make it well adapted to travel in harsh desert conditions. Be sure to include information about the animal's anatomy, diet, hair, and so on. Your report should include answers to the following questions: What is the average lifespan of the camel? What makes it different from the other creatures that dwell in the desert? How is the camel useful to humans living or traveling in the desert?

Project and Report Ideas

Natural Resources Map

On a map of Libya, use a key to show where the country's oil fields, olive groves, and date tree orchards are located. This information can be found on a map of Libya on the Internet or in an encyclopedia.

Archeological Report

Libya is an ancient land that contains many ruins from the days of bygone empires. Write a one-page report on one of the following cities:

- Sabratha
- Leptis Magna
- Germa
- Ptolemais

Biographies

Write a one-page report on one of the following figures in Libya's history:

- Eratosthenes
- Lucius Septimus Severus
- Italo Balbo
- King Idris I
- Omar Mukhtar
- Muammar al-Gadhafi

Chronology

ca. 1000 B.C.: Phoenicians settle in the Tripolitania region in western Libya.

631 B.C.: Greeks found the city of Cyrene and begin colonization along the eastern coast of the region later known as Cyrenaica.

ca. 400 B.C.: Carthage conquers Tripolitania.

74 B.C.: Romans conquer Libya and build vast cities, including Leptis Magna.

A.D. 455: Germanic tribe known as the Vandals takes control of Libya.

500s: Libya is absorbed into the Byzantine Empire.

642: Arabs invade Cyrenaica, bringing the Islamic religion to the region.

1500s: Libya is absorbed into the Ottoman Empire. The three provinces of Tripolitania, Cyrenaica, and Fezzan are governed from the capital city of Tripoli.

1911–12: Italian forces conquer Tripolitania and Cyrenaica and make the regions colonies.

1920s: Omar al-Mukhtar leads strong Libyan resistance to Italian rule.

1942: During World War II the Italians are forced from Libya.

1951: Libya becomes an independent nation; Mohammed Idris Al-Senussi is named king.

1959: Vast reserves of oil are discovered in the Surt Basin of Libya.

1961: Important oil fields in the interior of Libya are linked by pipeline to the Mediterranean Sea, making it possible for Libya to begin exporting oil.

1969: Colonel Muammar Al-Gadhafi leads a military coup during which King Idris's government is overthrown.

1977: Gadhafi launches his "people's revolution," which includes changing the country's official name from the Libyan Arab Republic to the Socialist People's Libyan Arab Jamahiriya.

1981: Two Libyan aircraft are shot down by U.S. forces after the Libyans challenge American warplanes flying over the Gulf of Sidra.

1982: United States imposes trade restrictions against Libya.

1984: Construction of the Great Man-Made River begins.

1986: In response to alleged Libyan involvement in the bombing of a Berlin discotheque frequented by American military personnel, the United States carries out bombing raids on Libyan military facilities and residential areas in Tripoli and Benghazi.

1988: In December, a bomb planted by Libyan terrorists explodes aboard Pan Am Flight 103 over Lockerbie, Scotland, killing 270 people.

1992: United Nations and U.S. government impose sanctions on Libya.

1999: Gadhafi turns over the suspects wanted for Pam Am Flight 103 trial.

2003: In August, Libya agrees to pay $2.7 billion to families of those killed in the Flight 103 bombing; the following month, the United Nations Security Council votes to lift sanctions. In December, Gadhafi announces that Libya will discontinue its nuclear weapons programs.

2004: Libya agrees to pay $35 million to the families of those killed in the 1986 Berlin disco bombing.

2006: In May, the United States and Libya restore full diplomatic ties.

2007: Six medical professionals are convicted of infecting hundreds of Libyan children with HIV.

Further Reading/Internet Resources

Diagram Group. *History of North Africa*. New York: Facts on File, 2003.

Miller, Debra. *Modern Nations of the World–Libya*. San Diego, Calif: Lucent Books, 2005.

Naden, Corrine and Rose Blue. *Heroes & Villains: Muammar al-Qaddafi*. San Diego, Calif.: Lucent Books, 2004.

Willis, Terry. *Enchantment of the World: Libya*. Danbury, Conn.: Children's Press, 1999.

Travel Information

http://lexicorient.com/libya/
http://www.lonelyplanet.com/worldguide/destinations/africa/libya/
http://travel.guardian.co.uk/countries/information/0,8766,-118,00.html

History and Geography

http://www.nationsencyclopedia.com/Africa/Libya.html
https://www.cia.gov/cia/publications/factbook/geos/ly.html#Intro
http://www.arab.net/libya/

Economic and Political Information

http://www.mathaba.net/info/
http://allafrica.com/libya/
http://www.zawya.com/countries/ly/

Culture and Festivals

http://www.pbs.org/wgbh/pages/frontline/shows/muslims/
http://www.libyana.org/
http://www.libyamazigh.org/
http://www.libya-watanona.com/libya1/

For More Information

Libyan Liaison Office
2600 Virginia Avenue NW
Suite 705
Washington, DC 20037
Tel: 202-944-9601

Mission of Libya to the United Nations
309 East 48th Street
New York, New York 10017
Tel: 212-752-5775
E-mail: lbyun@undp.org

U.S. Department of State
Bureau of Consular Affairs
2201 C Street NW
Washington, DC 20520
Tel: 202-647-4000

United States Embassy Tripoli
Corinthia Bab Africa Hotel
Souq At-Tlat Al-Qadim
Tripoli, Libya
Tel: 218-21-335-1848
E-mail: tripoliirm@state.gov
Website: http://libya.usembassy.gov/

Index

Numbers in **bold italic** refer to captions.

Contributors/Picture Credits

Professor Robert I. Rotberg is Director of the Program on Intrastate Conflict and Conflict Resolution at the Kennedy School, Harvard University, and President of the World Peace Foundation. He is the author of a number of books and articles on Africa, including *A Political History of Tropical Africa* and *Ending Autocracy, Enabling Democracy: The Tribulations of Southern Africa.*

Judy L. Hasday, a native of Philadelphia, Pennsylvania, received her bachelor of arts degree in communications and her master's degree in education from Temple University. Ms. Hasday has written dozens of books for young adults, including the New York Public Library Books for the Teen Age award winners *James Earl Jones* (1999) and *The Holocaust* (2003, 2004), and the National Social Studies Council 2001 Notable Social Studies Trade Book for Young People award winner *Extraordinary Women Athletes*. Her free time is devoted to music, photography, travel, volunteerism, and her pets—cat Sassy and four zebra finches.